THE
CALIFORNIA
MISSIONS

THE CALIFORNIA MISSIONS

ELIZABETH
VAN STEENWYK

A First Book
Franklin Watts
New York/Chicago/London/Toronto/Sydney

Cover photograph copyright ©: Ben Klaffke
Photographs copyright ©: Ben Klaffke: pp. 2, 18, 28, 35, 38, 41, 45, 49, 53; North
Wind Picture Archives: pp. 8, 10, 11, 32, 47; The Bettmann Archive: pp. 13, 44;
University of Southern California Library: p. 14; Archive Photos: pp. 16 (American
Stock), 21; Hubert A. Lowman: pp. 24, 27; Mission San Luis Rey Museum: p. 30;
San Diego Historical Society, Photograph Collection: p. 39.

Library of Congress Cataloging-in-Publication Data

Van Steenwyk, Elizabeth.
The California missions / Elizabeth Van Steenwyk.
p.   cm. — (A First book)
Includes bibliographical references and index.
ISBN 0-531-20187-2 (lib bdg.)   0-531-15893-4 (pbk.)
1. Indians of North America—Missions—California—Juvenile literature.
2. Missions—California—History—Juvenile literature.   3. Church architecture—
California—Juvenile literature.   4. Spain—Colonies—America—Administration—
Juvenile literature.   [1. Indians of North America—Missions—California.
2. Missions—California—History.]   I. Title.   II. Series.
E78.C15V14   1995
979.4'02—dc20   95–3847   CIP   AC

CONTENTS

A SACRED EXPEDITION

In 1493, shortly after Christopher Columbus returned to Spain from his first voyage of discovery, the leader of the Roman Catholic Church, Pope Alexander VI, divided the Americas into two spheres of exploration. He assigned all the land west of the dividing line, including the newly discovered "Indies," to Spain and all the land east to Portugal. Then he said that all further explorations be led by "worthy, God-fearing, learned, skilled

Christopher Columbus meets with his patrons, King Ferdinand and Queen Isabella. His first voyage of discovery was the beginning of Spanish colonization in America.

and experienced men in order to instruct the inhabitants in the Catholic faith."

During the sixteenth century, Spanish colonizing in the Americas was rapid and successful. It was accomplished with military might and religious zeal in present-day Mexico, Central America, the Caribbean, and part of South America.

The area that was then called California was another matter. Spain laid claim to it when navigator Juan Cabrillo discovered San Diego Bay in 1542. Without established land routes or nearby supply bases, California remained undisturbed for some years. But when Russia and England began to show interest in claiming the land for their own, Spain was moved to action.

In an effort to reestablish claim on Upper or Alta California, the king of Spain, Charles III, ordered the military to secure it for the Crown. In addition, a leader from the Franciscan order of the Catholic Church, Father Junípero Serra, was asked to create a chain of missions to help convert the local Indian peoples to Christianity.

Ultimately, Spain's efforts to colonize and spread Christianity resulted in the building of twenty-one missions along the coastal area of what is now the state of California. All of those missions, in some form of restoration, stand today.

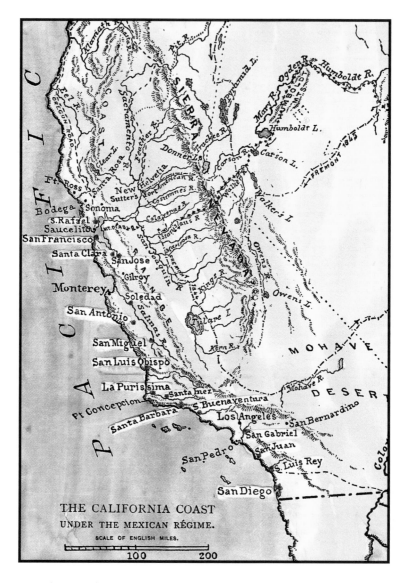

THE CALIFORNIA COAST
UNDER THE MEXICAN RÉGIME.

SCALE OF ENGLISH MILES.

100   200

This early map of the California coast shows only some of the missions that make up the chain from San Francisco to San Diego.

The Founding
of the Missions

Chapter

One

THE MISSIONS BEGIN

One day in late June 1769, a dusty mule train from Mexico, or New Spain as it was then called, led by Father Junípero Serra and Gaspar de Portolá, governor of California, neared San Diego Bay. The fifty-five-year-old *padre* was looking forward to reuniting the exploration parties that had left Mexico months before. When everyone gathered, he found that of the 219 original members in the party, only about half were left.

Father Junípero Serra

One ship was lost, many men had deserted or died, and the survivors were ill with scurvy from a lack of fresh fruit and vegetables.

Despite the bleak situation, Father Serra proceeded with plans to build a chain of missions. The *padre*, weak and suffering from an infected leg, roused the remaining men to work. Together, they built an *enramada*, or crude shelter, of brushwood. Then, gray-robed Father

Serra raised the cross within the simple shelter, celebrated Mass, and dedicated *Mission San Diego de Alcala*.

The American Indians who watched from a distance were suspicious of these strangers who arrived in "floating houses" and rode on the backs of unfamiliar animals. The Indians accepted gifts of beads and clothing, but refused offers of food. Before long, they became bold, tried to steal supplies, and even attacked the sick men. A protective stockade was quickly constructed around the crude mission and the Indians were driven away.

After planting the Spanish flag beside the *enramada*, Portolá headed north. He wanted to find Monterey Bay and secure that land for the Crown as well. When he returned to San Diego months later, Portolá was

Gaspar de Portolá, the governor of both Alta (or Upper) and Baja (or Lower) California, led expeditions that paved the way for the establishment of Franciscan missions.

convinced he had failed, but everyone was too weak and hungry to care. Finally, a ship bearing food arrived from Mexico. Within weeks, Father Serra left on the same ship to find the bay Portolá thought he had missed.

Portolá, his men, and another Franciscan friar, Juan Crespí, traveled overland and met the ship bearing Father Serra near where Portolá had placed a cross on his earlier journey. Certain that he had indeed found Monterey Bay, Portolá claimed the land for Spain, and in 1770 the second mission was founded. After bells were hung on some tree branches and an altar erected under a giant oak, uniformed troops and sailors gathered to listen to the *padre* bless the new Spanish mission.

The group soon completed a *presidio*, or fort, and a rustic mission. After turning over military authority to Lieutenant Pedro Fages, Portolá returned to New Spain. Before long, Fages began to interfere with the mission leadership and within months Father Serra had him removed by the viceroy of New Spain, the king's representative there. Fages did return to California later as a governor of the province, but tense relations between the mission's *padres* and military protectors continued.

Within a year, without enough land or water for irrigation, Father Serra moved the Monterey Bay mission to beautiful Carmel Valley, "two gunshots" or 2,400 to 2,800 feet (730 to 850 m) from the sea. It

Also known as the Carmel mission, Mission San Carlos Borromeo has two unusual architectural features for a mission: a domed bell tower (left side) and an arched, instead of flat, church ceiling.

became *Mission San Carlos Borromeo del Rio Carmelo* and headquarters for Father Serra. To protect the first two missions better, the Spaniards began colonizing the land between them.

With builders busy at work on a mission in Carmel, Father Serra set out to find a spot in the Santa Lucia Mountains that Portolá had seen months earlier. After a strenuous hike of 25 Spanish leagues or approximately 75 miles (120 km), Serra and his party stopped in a wooded area near a river, which he named Rio de San Antonio. On a summer day in 1771, Father Serra dedicated *Mission San Antonio de Pádua*. That day many Indians, friendly and eager to help, approached the rustic hut with acorns, pine nuts, and seeds.

Two weeks later, Father Serra returned to Carmel, leaving two other friars in charge of the newest mission. One of them, Father Buenaventura Sitjar, remained for thirty-seven years, during which time he directed the building of an aqueduct to tranport water from a river some miles away, a water-powered mill, and even a fountain. He also wrote a four-hundred-page vocabulary manual of the Mitsun language, spoken by the local Indian population.

Although Father Serra chose the site of the next mission, *Mission San Gabriel Arcángel*, two other *padres* actually dedicated it. During their trip from San Diego, the *padres* and their men met angry Indians. Hoping to prevent an attack, one of the holy men displayed a ban-

This ornate statue of the Virgin Mary from an altar in Mission San Gabriel Arcángel was brought from Spain in 1791.

ner of the Virgin Mary. The Indians dropped their weapons and placed bead necklaces before it. Greatly relieved, the founding party quickly moved on, built a shelter near a stream, and founded a mission in September 1771.

When spring floods ruined crops four years later, Father Fermín Francisco de Lasuén moved the mission to its present site. The mission was soon producing profitable crops of grain and grapes and serving as a stopping-off place for the frequent visitors who traveled the nearby trails. It became known as the "The Queen of the Missions."

It was Portolá's group who unknowingly led Father Serra to the site of the fifth mission. During their search for Monterey Bay in 1769, they came upon a grassy valley and hordes of grizzly bears looking for food. After feasting on some of the bears, the men named the area La Cañada de los Osos (Valley of the Bears). Soon, a hunting party from the missions came to the valley to scout for food. The hunters later sent back several tons of bear meat to the needy missions. Passing through on his way to San Diego, Father Serra chose for a mission site the valley where food was so plentiful and the Indians friendly. He dedicated *Mission San Luis Obispo de Tolosa* near two streams.

While looking for Monterey Bay in 1769, Portolá stumbled onto San Francisco Bay. After recognizing the importance of the discovery, the viceroy of New Spain resolved to build a *presidio* and send families to settle it for Spain. Lieutenant Colonel Juan Bautista de Anza, who had traveled the deserts and mountains of Upper or Alta California, led an overland party with Father Francisco Palou as its religious leader. On the return trip, De Anza brought four new passengers. The San Diego and San Gabriel missions, overrun with mice, had requested two cats each.

On June 29, 1776, five days before the Declaration of Independence was adopted, Father Palou offered the first Mass at *Mission San Francisco de Asis.* De Anza discovered a nearby stream and named it Arroyo de los Dolores and soon the mission became known as Mission Dolores.

The blustery and chilly climate of the location was not ideal for people or farming. In 1782, Father Palou moved the mission and the city of San Francisco grew up around it. When the earthquake of 1906 hit, the mission remained standing while larger and stronger buildings tumbled to the ground.

Mission San Juan Capistrano was founded twice. The first effort was abandoned because of conflicts with Indians at the San Diego mission. Father Serra headed the second founding party, erected a small chapel, and dedicated it on an autumn day in 1776.

The small house of worship was soon outgrown and an extension was completed in 1806. Only six years later, an earthquake reduced the huge building to rubble in minutes. The tired missionaries and their followers returned to the original chapel and left the great pile of ruin as a testimony to nature's power. The Serra Chapel is thought to be the only surviving structure in California where Father Serra led services.

The viceroy of New Spain ordered the missionaries to build a second San Francisco Bay mission to ward off attacks. *Mission Santa Clara de Asis* was the first named

This corridor of ancient arches and weathered tiles is located alongside the Serra Chapel at Mission San Juan Capistrano.

after a woman, St. Clare of Assissi, the founder of an order of nuns who took vows of absolute poverty. When the settlers found a rapidly flowing creek near the Guadalupe River, about 40 miles (64 km) southeast of Mission Dolores, they built an *enramada* and dedicated the eighth mission in January 1777.

Father Serra had long been eager to establish a third mission between San Diego and Carmel near the Santa Barbara Channel, but he had to wait more than twelve years. The reason for the delay reached all the way back to Spain, which was involved in costly European wars at the time. The king lacked the funds to support the *padres* and their missions and concluded that white settlers could colonize as easily and more cheaply. After several talks in Mexico City, Father Serra finally convinced Governor Felipe de Neve to approve two more missions and one *presidio*.

The first agreed-upon mission was dedicated on Easter Sunday morning in 1782, with Mass sung by the frail, elderly Father Serra. *Mission San Buenaventura* was successful from the beginning and had crops so abundant that whaling ships stopped regularly to take on cargoes of fruits and vegetables.

Although the *presidio* at Santa Barbara was built without delay, construction of the second mission was more complicated. Governor de Neve felt that the system gave too much power to the *padres* and blocked economic support for another mission. Father Serra waited anxiously for work to begin, but nothing happened. Sadly, he returned to Carmel. Finally, the viceroy reversed the governor's decision and approved funding for *Mission Santa Bárbara*. On August 28, 1784, a month after hearing that the tenth mission would be built after all, Father Serra died.

Chapter

Two

THE WORK CONTINUES

Father Lasuén became the next president of the missions and vowed to finish the work Father Serra had begun. His first project, the mission at Santa Bárbara, was dedicated on December 4, 1786. The mission attracted so many Indian settlers that extra buildings were built and it was soon a small village, with the most complete water system of all the missions. In fact, the city of Santa Barbara still uses the reservoir and dam today.

This statue from Mission San Gabriel Arcángel illustrates the relationship between the padres and their Indian followers. This relationship could be interpreted as caring and paternal or harsh and oppressive.

Father Lasuén dedicated the eleventh mission, *Mission La Purísima Concepción* in December 1787, less than three months after the signing of the U.S. Constitution. The mission thrived in the fertile valley until a tremendous earthquake in 1812 completely shattered the church and nearby buildings. The *padres* quickly built a finer mission some miles away from the old site. Drought, fire, and revolt by some Indians contributed to the mission's decline. Soon, only a few fragments of wall remained to remind anyone a mission once stood there.

The next mission, *Mission Santa Cruz*, was dedicated in 1791. With a favorable location, rich soil, and a warm climate, it seemed set to succeed, but for many reasons, never did.

Although Spanish law forbade *pueblos* to be within one league or roughly 3 miles (5 km) of a mission, Branciforte, named after the viceroy, was settled across the river from the mission. More troubling, the *pueblo* was home to dishonest settlers who stole freely from the missions. One day, the ship of a notorious pirate, Hyppolyte de Bouchard, who had attacked settlements as near as Monterey, was sighted offshore. The *padres* rushed to pack the mission's valuables and store them inland. The citizens of Branciforte, instead of helping, looted the mission. After the pirate ship had passed and the *padres* returned, they found little left for their community. Its converts and religious leaders disheartened, the mission faded away.

During Portolá's search for Monterey Bay in 1769, he came across yet another site for a mission. He and his weary men camped in a dry, desolate spot near the Salinas River and soon learned why the area was so uninhabited. In fact, when an Indian was asked his name, his answer sounded like *soledad*, the Spanish word for "loneliness." It fit the locale and when Father Lasuén dedicated the mission in 1791, he named it *Mission Nuestra Señora de la Soledad*, or Our Lady of Solitude.

Mission life at Our Lady of Solitude proceeded at a leisurely pace. It took six years to build a permanent church and with so few Indians in the area, the population grew slowly. After the *padres* learned how to use the Salinas River for irrigating crops and feeding the animals, life improved. Then a widespread epidemic, floods, and bad weather brought despair to the mission community and many left altogether. The mission roofs were sold to pay a debt to the Mexican government. Soon, only crumbling remnants of the mission remained.

Finally, Father Lasuén appealed to the viceroy of New Spain to fund the missions. He argued that it was less expensive to support missions than military escorts for supply caravans to and from California. The government agreed and authorized money to build five new missions.

The first one, *Mission San José de Guadalupe*, was dedicated on a site east of the southern tip of San Francisco Bay in 1797. Soon cattle and sheep arrived

These are the remains of the massive stone walls that were once part of the original Mission Nuestra Señora de la Soledad.

from the Santa Clara Mission and the small group held a fiesta and a barbecue to celebrate.

Only thirteen days after dedicating the San José mission, Father Lasuén founded the *Mission San Juan Bautista*. Unfortunately, the mission sat on a major fracture of the San Andreas fault. When an earthquake leveled the church, it had to be rebuilt. Almost immediately, plans were made to replace it with a larger church.

Tireless Father Lasuén founded a third mission in the summer of 1797. Attendance was high and fifteen Indian children were baptized at the dedication of

Fresco painting is an art form in which artists apply paint directly to fresh plaster. This fresco at Mission San Miguel Arcángel is seen as it was originally painted; it has never been restored.

Mission San Miguel Arcángel, which immediately prospered. One *padre*, Father Juan Martin, taught the local artisans to make bricks for the new church. When it was finished, a Spanish artist, Esteban Munras, designed and painted the interior including the *reredos*, or wall behind the altar. The San Miguel Church is considered to be the only mission containing its original artwork.

At sixty-one years old, Father Lasuén set to work on building his fourth mission in a four-month period in 1797. The new mission was located in a valley called Encino, near the growing *pueblo* of Los Angeles. It closed the gap between the San Gabriel and San Buenaventura missions along *El Camino Reál*, which is Spanish for "The Royal Road." *Mission San Fernando Rey de España* flourished after its founding in September.

Later, after gold was discovered on the property, settlers searched for the "dead monks'" treasure in their spare time. When gold was discovered in 1848 at Sutter's Mill in central California, prospectors rushed north and the hunt for gold in the San Fernando mission district was abandoned. The city of Los Angeles, however, expanded and attracted visitors. The mission was soon popular as a convenient overnight stop and rooms were added to accommodate travelers who brought tales of adventure and excitement to the isolated mission.

The ninth and final mission that Father Lasuén founded, *Mission San Luis Rey de Francia*, in 1798, closed the gap between San Diego and San Juan Capistrano. At over 6 acres (2 ha), it occupied the most area, and served the largest population of all the missions. The mission's growth was credited to Father Antonio Peyri, who was present at the founding ceremony and stayed for thirty-four years.

Energetic and organized, Father Peyri was able to bring projects to completion swiftly. A unique water system supported a bathing pond and *lavandería*, or

This photograph of Mission San Luis Rey was taken in 1892. The foundations of Father Peyri's water system and lavandería are in the foreground.

laundry, built below the mission and from which water flowed to irrigate the fields. Father Peyri also directed the planting of fruit trees, vegetable gardens, and vineyards, and the building of a winery.

When Father Peyri left the mission, tradition has it that five hundred mission Indians followed him to San Diego to beg him to come back. They arrived as he was sailing out of the harbor, but he blessed them from his ship. He returned to Spain, knowing that mission life in California as he knew it would soon end.

Chapter

Three

THE MISSIONS MARCH ON

The year after Father Lasuén's death in 1803, his successor, Father Estévan Tápis, founded *Mission Santa Inés*, the third dedicated to a woman. Built in a beautiful valley 45 miles (72 km) northwest of the Santa Barbara mission, it was called the "hidden gem of the missions" because visitors had to climb rocky, dusty hills to reach it. The original church, completed in

The missions, usually no more than a comfortable day's horseback ride apart, were convenient gathering places for those traveling up or down the California coast.

1812, was demolished by an earthquake that same year and work started quickly on another one.

Trouble of another nature came to the mission when Mexican soldiers and Indians began to quarrel. The quarrels erupted into fights and a fire that almost destroyed the mission church until the Indians pitched in to help save it.

At the large missions, farming activities could take the Indian workers far from the church center. The *padres* built small ranchos with chapels, or *asistencias* for them to live and worship more easily when they were away from the missions. Eventually, twenty *asistencias* were established to complement the chain of missions.

The twentieth mission, *Mission San Rafael Arcángel*, actually began as an *asistencia* of Mission Dolores. The bay mission had such damp weather that many Indian followers became ill. The *padres* sent them to a sunny site across the bay to recuperate and named it after the archangel whose name means "healing power of God." The Indians soon recovered, and the *asistencia* thrived as well. San Rafael was dedicated in 1817 and given full mission status five years later. Its church, one of the simplest, architecturally, of all the mission churches was in use for only ten years before it was abandoned.

Interestingly, the last Franciscan mission, *Mission San Francisco Solano*, was established without church approval. After obtaining permission from the governor, José Altimira, an unpopular *padre* who flogged the Indians and ultimately returned to Spain, founded the mission in 1823. That same year, President James Monroe proclaimed the Monroe Doctrine, which opposed any expansion of European control in the western hemisphere, including the United States.

Fifty-four years after Father Serra held Mass in the first *enramada*, the mission chain was complete. The Spanish dream of settling Alta California had come true, but its control over that land would be short-lived.

Mission Life

Chapter

One

HOMEMADE MISSIONS

When the Franciscan fathers and Spanish explorers came from New Spain to begin the mission chain, they brought food, clothing, and tools overland and by sea. They were unable, however, to carry building supplies on the long, hazardous journey to California and had to use what was on hand. Carefully, they selected sites near Indian populations, a river or the ocean, as well as fertile soil, and ample timber when possible. Then it was time to build the missions.

The first temporary missions were built of sticks, brush, mud, and *tule*, or reeds, for the roofs. The mission walls at Carmel, for example, were made of pine trees, stripped and trimmed, with rocks and rubble to fill in the spaces. The roof was made with pine and cypress beams, covered with poles and straw, and filled with clay and mud. Since no nails were available, they had to lash all the poles and beams together with rawhide. Later, gabled roofs, covered with thatch, were added, but they were unable keep out the wind and rain, and fire was a constant worry.

The permanent mission buildings were constructed of *adobe* bricks. *Adobe* refers to clay, mixed with straw and sometimes manure, poured into molds and dried in the sun. The *adobe* walls were then covered with a plaster made of limestone, sand, and water. When it dried, it offered protection from the rain.

The roofs, however, were still leaky, drafty, and dangerous. The *padres* had tried for some time to duplicate the red-tiled roofs of their native Spain. Finally, after getting the right mixture of clay and water, they pressed it over curved, wooden forms until dry, removed the forms, and fired the tiles in a kiln, or oven. When the tiles were removed from the kiln, they were red and fire retardant.

Mission San Antonio's new church was covered with red tiles in 1776, becoming the first building in the province to be roofed with this material. Then red-tiled roofs were quickly added to the buildings at *Mission San Luis Obispo* after three devastating fires nearly wiped it out. Soon the *padres* and the Indians at *Mission San Diego* began to manufacture *tejas*, or roof tiles, for all the missions on a regular basis.

Ladrillos, or floor bricks, were made in squares of a thicker, heavier clay mixture than the *tejas*. They were also baked in kilns after drying in the sun. Some of the tiles have footprints from animals walking on the squares before they had completely dried.

To prevent attack from colonists from other countries or unfriendly Indians, the missions were laid out in a quadrangle around a patio, or courtyard. The quadrangle also kept the Indians confined once they had converted to the mission way of life. Of all twenty-one

The mission builders packed clay mixed with straw into a mold to make adobe bricks.

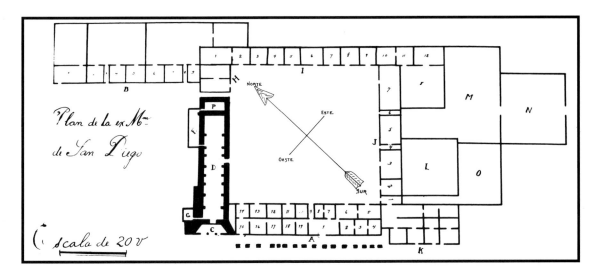

*This floor plan for Mission San Diego
illustrates the typical quadrangle layout
for the majority of the missions.*

missions, only one, *Mission La Purísima*, failed to follow the quadrangle pattern. The mission was constructed almost in a straight line, with the idea that it would be safer in an earthquake.

The *padres* planned each mission to accommodate three types of activities: religious, residential, and work. The church was the most important and often occupied the northeast corner of the quadrangle. The *padres* lived in a building in the quadrangle called the *convento*. The men and women were housed in buildings called the *monjeriá*—one for the girls, unmarried women, and married women whose husbands were away, and one for the unmarried men and boys. The servants' quarters, workshops, and storerooms were also in the quadrangle. Outside the quadrangle was the Indian village, with separate houses for families, the guards' quarters, and sometimes workshops such as the tannery and pottery. The land surrounding the quadrangle was often used for growing crops.

The missions themselves recalled some of the building styles in Spain and Mexico where the *padres* used to live and work. However, most of the missions were built in a simple way for a simple reason.

Neither the *padres* nor the Indians who came to help them were trained engineers, architects, or builders. They learned as they went along. The mission walls, for example, had to be built thick and low, because the *adobe* bricks, while heavy, were not strong and could not bear much weight. In turn, the walls could support roof beams of only a certain length, which determined the width of the entire building. And the *adobe* bricks often dissolved in heavy rains, so the *padres* added wide eaves and arched corridors to preserve the walls. Although these architectural details were developed for practical reasons, they were eventually appreciated in their own right.

Artistans trained in Europe or the Americas added other design features to some of the missions. Decorations gave doors and windows more elegance

The stone carving is from Mission San Juan Capistrano. The cross and bell is from Mission Santa Inés.

and importance. False fronts, called *espadañas*, made the mission churches seem taller and more regal. Walls with cutouts for hanging bells, or *campanarios*, could be seen, and the bells heard, for miles to guide visitors to the mission. Inside the churches, frescoes were decorated with paint made from local materials. Wood carvings, stone, and ironwork, some directed by more experienced artists, were actually completed by the *padres* and Indians who showed remarkable skill and appreciation of color.

Before real window glass arrived in California, the mission workers made temporary coverings. They stretched cowhide over wooden frames and shaved and greased the hides to make them translucent. The frames were then nailed into wall openings during cold weather to keep out wind and rain and let in some sunlight during the day.

The so-called mission architecture has been copied over the years for churches, homes, and schools and also for some commercial buildings. The much-loved mission design, however, grew out of a simple need for shelter, built from local materials.

Chapter

Two

LIFE INSIDE THE MISSIONS

The missions were meant to be a center for agricultural, industrial, and educational as well as religious activity. Once built, each mission became a small, but active, walled city with two entrances, which were closed at night to keep out raiders and confine the Indians.

The mission residents stirred at first light as the tolling bells called everyone to chapel and then to breakfast. The *padres* often ate bread and chocolate for

*Mission life was structured and busy for the padres
and their Indian followers.*

their first meal and the Indians ate a porridge called
atole made from ground roasted corn or grain. Then
everyone went to work at their assigned jobs.

The Indians worked and excelled as bakers, cooks,
carpenters, winemakers, tanners, shepherds, candlemak-
ers, tilemakers, horticulturists, and musicians, among
other trades. At noon, another bell called the Indians and
padres together for a meal and a *siesta*, or nap. Then they

all returned to work in the kitchen, fields, workshops, or stables until about five o'clock, when it was time for church. The evening meal was at six o'clock.

In the evenings, there were lessons in music, the Spanish language, Christian teachings, and recreation. Sometimes the Indians performed their traditional dances and songs celebrating acorn harvests or good hunting. A visitor's arrival often prompted festivities such as the one at *Mission San Luis Obispo*, which fea-

Music was an important part of life at the missions. Some padres taught the Indians choral music. Shown is an early mission choir book.

tured a bullfight, mission-style. At the end of the evening, instead of killing the bull, the participants rolled it over in the dust.

Many of the *padres* contributed to cultural as well as religious life at the missions. Father Felipe del Arroyo de la Cuesta from the *Mission San Juan Bautista* could communicate in any of several Indian languages. A *padre* at the San José mission, Narciso Durán, was a skilled music instructor. Although he was not formally trained, he organized a thirty-piece band and taught the Indians to play homemade instruments. People came from miles around to hear the mission concerts.

Father Estévan Tápis, another talented musician, introduced a system of colored notes to teach the singing parts. The Indian boys' choir that he directed became famous in the area. Once, the mission's barrel organ so entranced a group of battling Tulare Indians that they threw down their weapons and stayed to hear more music.

When it was time to go to sleep, the Indian families went to their sections of the long *monjeriás* or to their small houses outside the compound. After the bedtime bell rang, they climbed ladders to the sleeping quarters of the *monjeriá*. The ladders were then removed and returned in the morning.

Before their mission days, the California Indians were hunter-gatherers, eating only what grew or lived naturally around them. More than five hundred kinds of food made out of plants and animals from the wild pro-

When the Spaniards arrived in California, they found Indian cultures rich in religious beliefs, artistry, and craftsmanship.

vided the Indians a complete and nutritional diet. For instance, acorns had more calories than wheat or barley and were ground into meal for bread, tortillas, or mush. Large and small game, fish, and shellfish from the ocean or nearby streams were all good sources of protein.

The Indians might have found it strange to work the land in such an unfamiliar way, clearing, plowing, and growing crops. But they learned quickly as they saw results. Soon they harvested crops of wheat and barley, vegetables, fruits, and even flowers. Hollyhocks, which the *padres* called St. Joseph's Staff, were a favorite in mission gardens. Under the direction of the *padres* and their own hard work, the Indians cultivated thousands of acres.

The Indians who lived in California spoke many dialects and were as unique as their spoken words. Some groups, such as the Chumash, who lived along the Santa Barbara Channel, possessed technologically developed skills. These people were accomplished canoe builders and basket weavers whose abilities were much admired by the Spaniards. Some tribes were part-time farmers while some, unable to thrive as hunter-gatherers, lived a meager existence. Still other Indian groups, east of the Sierra Nevada mountains, such as the Mojaves, had weapons of war.

The American Indians were originally attracted to the missions out of curiosity and interest in gifts from the *padres.* The Indians were never forced to join the missions or accept Christianity, but once they did, they were

This wall painting is from Mission San Antonio and depicts an Indian carving a statue of the Madonna. While the mission system brought some positive changes to the Indian way of life, the loss of Indian traditions was great.

expected to live by mission rules and Spanish law. After entering mission life, they had to remain within the mission community, work at an assigned job, and follow the Catholic faith. Just as a Spanish citizen was unable to renounce Catholicism, neither could an American Indian.

If an Indian did try to run away from a mission, Spanish soldiers brought him back and punished him, as Spanish law required. The soldiers assigned to the *presidios* often mistreated the Indians and their families and were punished for it. In the missions, flogging or a term in prison, shackles, or the stocks were doled out for Indians and Spanish citizens alike.

Some American Indians were content with their new mission life and some weren't. Some say that missions were good for the Indians, that most *padres* treated them kindly and prepared them for a life that soon would surround them as more settlers poured into the area. Others say that accepting mission life was a form of slavery that forced Indians to give up their heritage and work at trades that were against their beliefs. Further, the white man's world brought diseases against which the local people had no immunity and thousands died as a result. Did the mission system treat the Indians fairly or exploit them? The issue is as controversial now as it was then.

Chapter

Three

SECULARIZATION AND RESTORATION

As Spanish colonies throughout the world became self-sufficient and Spain's power and influence faded, independence followed. In 1821, Mexico declared its independence from Spain and then claimed Alta California for its own. For years, a series of Mexican governors vied for power and land in the province. Finally, the Mexican government passed a bill in 1833 ordering all the missions to be secularized, or converted to civil control. Under this law, the Roman Catholic Church was to keep only the religious buildings and sacred items. The vast land holdings were to be divided between the neighboring *pueblos* and the American Indians, but it didn't happen exactly that way. Much of the valuable agricultural land and livestock was taken by civilian authorities or sold to settlers for little of its actual worth.

Thrown from their homes and unable to reinstate their former way of life, the mission Indians suffered. Some land was rightfully turned over to them, but they often lost ownership, or sometimes gambled it away. Many Indians were forced to work for the new landowners, some of whom treated them as virtual slaves.

In 1850, California joined the Union as a free state. Under the U.S. Land Commission, some mission buildings and land were returned to the Roman Catholic Church, which was unable to support all of it. Some of the buildings were rented out as hog barns, stores, private homes, or hotels. Over the years, the missions were neglected and in some cases, parts of the buildings were actually sold off.

Today, all twenty-one California missions have been restored and, in some cases, entirely rebuilt. These campanarios from Mission San Diego de Alcala were restored in 1931.

One building, however, survived through the years quite well. After the *padres* left, the chapel at *Mission San Juan Capistrano* served as a barn for storing hay. In an effort to keep his hay dry, a farmer rebuilt the roof. While the other mission buildings nearby crumbled to the ground, the chapel, with its protective roof, stood solid.

Around the turn of the century, artists discovered the striking mission ruins and began to etch, photograph, and paint them. The artwork stirred the public to work to restore the missions. They studied old records, drawings, and photographs to reconstruct buildings as close to the originals as possible. Each mission along *El Camino Reál*, open to the public, offers a meaningful look into this period of western American history.

A MISSION TIMELINE

Name	Founded
Mission San Diego de Alcala	July 16, 1769
Mission San Carlos Borromeo del Rio Carmelo	June 3, 1770
Mission San Antonio de Pádua	July 14, 1771
Mission San Gabriel Arcángel	September 8, 1771
Mission San Luis Obispo de Tolosa	September 1, 1772

Name	Founded
Mission San Francisco de Asis (known as Mission Dolores)	June 29, 1776
Mission San Juan Capistrano	November 1, 1776
Mission Santa Clara de Asis	January 12, 1777
Mission San Buenaventura	March 31, 1782
Mission Santa Bárbara	December 4, 1786
Mission La Purísima Concepción	December 8, 1787
Mission Santa Cruz	September 25, 1791
Mission Nuestra Señora de la Soledad (Our Lady of Solitude)	October 9, 1791
Mission San José de Guadalupe	June 11, 1797
Mission San Juan Bautista	June 24, 1797
Mission San Miguel Arcángel	July 25, 1797
Mission San Fernando Rey de España	September 8, 1797
Mission San Luis Rey de Francia	June 13, 1798
Mission Santa Inés	September 17, 1804
Mission San Rafael Arcángel	December 14, 1817
Mission San Francisco Solano	July 4, 1823

A GLOSSARY OF SPANISH TERMS

Adobe — a brick made of clay, mixed with straw and sometimes manure

Asistencia — a sub-mission or small ranch with chapels where mission followers could live and worship while tending mission animals and crops

Atole — a porridge or gruel made out of cornmeal

Campanario — a mission wall with cutouts for hanging bells

Convento — the building that housed the mission *padres*

El Camino Reál — The Royal Road, also called the King's Highway. It runs almost the length of California and links the mission chain. The present U.S. Highway 101 closely follows it.

Enramada — a shelter made of brush that housed the mission altar until a more permanent structure could be built

Espadaña — the false front of a mission church

Ladrillos — bricks used on floors

Lavandería — the mission laundry

Monjeriá — the men and women's quarters in the mission

Padre — a father or priest

Presidio — a fort in a place controlled by the Spanish

Pueblo — a town or village

Reredos — the decorated wall behind the church altar

Siesta — an afternoon nap

Tejas — roof tiles

Tule — a reed used to make shelters and roofs

FOR FURTHER INFORMATION

Mission San Diego de Alcala
10818 San Diego Mission Road
Mission Valley, CA 92108

Mission San Luis Rey de Francia
4050 Mission Avenue
San Luis Rey, CA 92068

Mission San Juan Capistrano
Ortega Highway & Camino
  Capistrano
San Juan Capistrano, CA 92675

Mission San Gabriel Arcangel
537 West Mission Drive
San Gabriel, CA 91776

San Fernando Rey de Espana
15151 San Fernando Mission
  Road
Mission Hills, CA 91345

Mission San Buenaventura
211 East Main Street
Ventura, CA 93001

Mission Santa Barbara
2201 Laguna Street
Santa Barbara, CA 93105

Mission Santa Ines
Highway 246
Solvang, CA 93463

Mission La Purisima
2295 Purisima Road
Lompoc, CA 93436

Mission San Luis Obispo de
  Tolosa
Monterey and Chorro Streets
San Luis Obispo, CA 93401

Mission San Miguel Arcangel
776 Mission Street
San Miguel, CA 93451

Mission San Antonio de Padua
Hunter Liggett Military
  Reservation
Jolon Road
Jolon, CA 93928

Carmel Mission Basilica
Rio and Lasuen Roads
Carmel, CA 93923

Mission Nuestra Senora de la
  Soledad

36641 Fort Romie Road
Soledad, CA 93960

Mission San Juan Bautista
Second and Mariposa Streets
San Juan Bautista, CA 95045

Mission Santa Cruz
126 High Street
Santa Cruz, CA 95060

Mission Santa Clara de Asis
Santa Clara University
500 El Camino Real
Santa Clara, CA 95050

Mission San Jose
43300 Mission Boulevard
Fremont, CA 94539

Mission San Francisco de Asis
  (or Mission Dolores)
3321 16th Street
San Francisco, CA 94114

Mission San Rafael Arcangel
1104 Fifth Avenue
San Rafael, CA 94901

Mission San Francisco Solano
114 East Spain Street
Sonoma, CA 95476

FOR FURTHER READING

Dolan, Sean. *Junípero Serra*. New York: Chelsea House, 1991.

Keyworth, C. L. *California Indians*. New York: Facts on File, 1990.

Lyngheim, Linda. *Indians and the California Missions*. Rev. ed. Van Nuys, Calif.: Langtry Publications, 1994.

Sinnott, Susan. *Extraordinary Hispanic Americans*. Chicago: Childrens Press, 1991.

Young, Stanley, and Melba Levic. *The Missions of California*. San Francisco: Chronicle Books, 1988.

INDEX

ABOUT THE AUTHOR

Elizabeth Van Steenwyk has written more than fifty books for young people, including the Franklin Watts First Books *California Gold Rush: West with the Forty-Niners* and *Frederic Remington*. She also wrote *Ida B. Wells-Barnett: Woman of Courage*, which was a NCSS/CBC Notable Children's Trade Book in the Field of Social Studies for 1992. Ms. Van Steenwyk lives with her husband in San Marino, California.